Quick Fixes
For Bored Kids

D1331916

Visit Tommy's website at:
www.wobblebottom.com/boredkids

Quick Fixes
For Bored Kids

Tommy Donbavand

How To Books

Published by How To Books Ltd,
3 Newtec Place, Magdalen Road,
Oxford OX4 1RE, United Kingdom.
Tel: (01865) 793806. Fax: (01865) 248780.
email: info@howtobooks.co.uk
www: http://www.howtobooks.co.uk

First published 2001
Reprinted 2001

British Library Cataloguing in Publication Data.

A catalogue record for this book is available from the British
Library.

Cover design by Shireen Nathoo Design, London
Cover illustration by Roger Langridge
Cartoons by Grizelda Grizlingham

Produced for How To Books by Deer Park Productions
Design and Typeset by Shireen Nathoo Design, London
Printed and Bound by Bell & Bain Ltd., Glasgow

NOTE: The material contained in this book is set out in good faith
for general guidance and no liability can be accepted for loss or
expense incurred as a result of relying in particular circumstances
on statements made in the book. Laws and regulations are
complex and liable to change, and readers should check the
current position with the relevant authorities before making
personal arrangements.

Contents

Preface

'I'm Bored'

How often has that cry echoed around your house on a long, rainy afternoon? Or from the back seat of the car while journeying to some distant day out?

Now those moans of desperation can be transformed into cheers of excitement with the ideas and suggestions contained within this book.

Whether you need to amuse a single child, or a whole party of school friends, there are dozens of unique activities for every occasion, and for every age group: from projects to make, through scavenger hunts, to madcap games – just dip in and beat those boredom blues!

And these fixes really are quick! With a little preparation, you'll have everything on hand for whenever boredom strikes, leaving you to get on with your day. Maximum entertainment with minimum effort.

So, switch off that TV set, and pull the plug on the games console. Here come activities that will pass your kids' time – at a thousand smiles an hour!

What's in the Box?

Pick up any other book of children's activities, and you'll find some great sounding ideas – until you read further.

Then, you're likely to be faced with a long list of materials that you can't begin the project without (try finding a tablespoon of alum for that playdough recipe on a wet Sunday evening...).

With these quick fixes, you'll never be stuck for an essential item – thanks to the **Boredom Box**! All you need is a sturdy cardboard box, and you're ready to go.

Each chapter will begin with a list of handy items to drop into the Boredom Box, ready for the activities that follow. But don't stop there. Every time you come across something that could have use in the future, add it to the box, and you'll have an instant collection of great activity materials.

Why not get your kids to decorate the Boredom Box with paints or coloured paper, and encourage them to add items of their own?

So, whenever boredom bites – the answer lies in the box!

Everyone's a Winner

One of the greatest challenges in entertaining children is morale. In today's competitive world, for every winner there is also a loser, and children can quickly become discouraged from continuing with an activity if they're not enjoying an element of success.

The way around this is with the **points system**.

Instead of declaring a winner, every child is awarded a number of points to add to an ongoing total. So, for example, at the end of a matchbox hunt, the child with the highest score is awarded 5 points, second place receives 4 points, and so on.

These points are tallied in each child's points book – which can be a small notepad, or a few sheets of paper folded and stapled.

An important factor is to ensure that the points count towards something. Perhaps your kids could trade them in at the end of the month for a special trip or gift? This will keep them working hard at the activities, and keeps that competitive edge without the need for winners and losers.

Encourage your children to invent a favourite theme for their points system, and decorate their books. Maybe it's a pirate club, where they're playing for gold doubloons rather than points? Or based around the jungle, adding paw prints to their books instead of numbers? The only limit is their imaginations.

Where to turn for more?

If you're connected to the Internet, there's a website that accompanies the book, full of links to great children's resources all over the world wide web. The site can be found at **www.wobblebottom.com/boredkids**, and you can email me with your questions or comments about the book at **boredkids@wobblebottom.com**

Now, let's banish some boredom...

Tommy Donbavand

About the Author

Tommy Donbavand has entertained children around the world for over 15 years, and now works in London as a writer and actor. He'd like to thank his parents for making sure he was never bored!

Chapter One

It's Raining Again!

THE BOREDOM BOX

Items to add to the box for this chapter:

*   an empty matchbox or stock cube box for each child

*   dough (or ingredients from the recipe below)

*   safety pins or magnets

*   a ball of wool and a reel of cotton

* face paint (or ingredients from the recipe below)

* pens and paper

* poster paints

* drinking straws

* sticky tape, drawing pins, or Blu-tack®

* sheets of newspaper.

Cold, Wet and Bored!

Why do the worst cases of boredom strike when it's raining outside, and kids are confined to the house? There's nothing on TV, they've read all their books and they've even finished their homework! Here are some quick fixes that guarantee a sunnier outlook!

Matchbox Hunt

Give each player an empty matchbox or
stock cube box.

At your signal, the players are given
exactly 30 minutes to cram as many items
as they can find around the house into the
box, and return to base.

There are a few basic rules to follow
during the hunt:

* only one of each item (2,000 grains of
  salt don't count!)

* only safe items (nothing from the
  medicine cabinet, etc.)

* items must fit inside the matchbox
  when closed.

The Big Count

When the 30 minutes are up, players meet back at the start, and lay out their items for counting on a sheet of newspaper.

The player with the most items is awarded the highest number of points, which then decrease for each player's total.

Now it's time to put it all back...

Star Struck

Every child has a favourite star – be it a member of a pop group, a film or TV actor, or a sports hero. Many of these celebrities will happily provide signed photographs, and in some cases, personal replies to letters. Collecting autographs and pictures is both rewarding and fun, and could develop into a hobby that lasts for years. But where do you start?

Find That Address

If you're contacting a TV star, write to the publicity department at their latest show, who will send out a signed picture, and pass the letter on to the star's agent.

In the case of sports stars, such as footballers, direct any requests for photographs to the player at their club.

Film and pop stars may take a little more tracking down. Write to the film studio or record company, or you could locate the star's agent and contact them there.

If you have Internet access, film and pop stars' contact addresses can be found at sites such as:

* www.addresses.site2go.com

* www.geocities.com/Hollywood/Hills/
  1835/

and a good site for music addresses:

* www.celebrityaddressbook.com

Never pay for addresses or signed photos.
Celebrities won't charge for autographs (if
they do, steer clear), and their contact info
will be available free elsewhere.

Take A Letter

Now your kids can write to their heroes,
and ask for a signed photo. They can tell
them how much they enjoyed their latest
film/CD/goal – celebrities respond well to

a little flattery!

If they're requesting a large number of pictures, it's polite to enclose a stamped self-addressed envelope, and if they're writing abroad, include an International Reply Coupon, available from post offices for 60p.

Dough Models

Here's a recipe for success – dough that can be used for modelling fun, then baked hard and painted to make items such as badges or fridge magnets. You will need (per child):

* 225g plain flour

* 115g table salt

* 125ml cold water.

Your kids should mix all the ingredients together well. If the mixture feels too sticky, knead in some extra flour. If too dry, add water a teaspoon at a time. When the dough becomes pliable, it's ready to model with.

Model Behaviour

Cover the floor around the table with sheets of newspaper, and make sure that the children are wearing aprons, or older clothes.

To make badges or fridge magnets, they should break off a small ball of the dough, and roll it around until soft and easily moulded. Then simply flatten the ball with the palm of their hand, and use the edge of a teaspoon to cut the dough into the desired shape.

Now They're Cooking!

When they have created all their models, place these in the oven on a high heat (200 degrees) for two to three hours, or until they start to turn brown and hard. The larger the items, the longer they'll need to bake. Remember to supervise children at all times while they're using the oven.

After baking, leave the creations to cool, then decorate, using poster paints.

When the paint is dry, they can glue a safety pin on the back for a badge, or a magnet to stick it to the fridge door.

Kids can experiment with other models and shapes, such as candle holders, or even picture frames. Ideal

Christmas or birthday presents for friends and family!

The Haunted Dungeon

A ghoulish way to spend a wet afternoon! Using items from the Boredom Box, and their imaginations, your kids must convert a bedroom into a haunted dungeon.

Boris The Spider

The main feature is a huge spider's web that covers an entire wall or, even better, the ceiling.

Get your kids to draw the pattern for the spider's web on paper first, so they will have something to work from. Then, using drawing pins, sticky tape or Blu-tack® they should fix lengths of wool to the wall, and create the outline for the web. If pins are being used, make sure to supervise.

Once they have the outline, criss-cross the wool between the outer points, and create the central pattern of the web.

If there is any wool left over, ball it up and stick eight drinking straws into it as legs to create the spider himself. Make some scary eyes from paper, and fix the spider to the edge of the web, waiting to pounce...

Decorate The Dungeon

Add some other scary features around the room:

* Dangle lengths of cotton from the doorframe – they'll feel like cobwebs in your face!

* Stuff clothes with pillows and blankets, and have a headless body in the bed.

* Cut a skeleton from sheets of newspaper, and hang it inside the wardrobe. Tie it to the handle with cotton, so that it jumps out when the door is opened!

Scary Sound Effects

If you have a cassette recorder, your kids
can make a tape of terrifying moans,
groans and ghostly sounds to play in the
background. See how many scary sounds
they can make with items from around
the house: dripping water, sounds of
ghostly footsteps, mysterious bumps and
bangs, and much more...

Little Horrors

To complete the effect, paint your kids' faces in scary designs with some home-made face paint. For each colour you will need:

* 1 teaspoon of water.

* 1 teaspoon of moisturising cream.

* 2 teaspoons of cornflour.

* food colouring.

Mix the cornflour with the water and moisturising cream in an old yoghurt pot. Add the food colouring a few drops at a time until you reach the desired colour. Then turn your kids into the monsters you always knew they were! The face paint washes off easily with soap and water.

Now it's time to invite friends and family into the haunted dungeon to discover all the scary surprises!

Blow Art

A quick and fun way to create unique art. Spread sheets of newspaper out first, and supervise young children.

Your kids should mix poster paints with a few teaspoons of water to make them nice and runny. Drip some of the paint onto a piece of paper then, using a drinking straw, blow the paint around.

They can create unusual shapes and patterns, and mix different colours by blowing them together. They can also tilt

the paper to make the paint run, or fold
the sheet in half to print the image. Leave
these to one side to dry.

Your kids can use their artwork to
create personalised greetings cards or party
invitations.

HINTS AND TIPS

* Use the matchbox hunt to explain the dangers of matches.

* Remind kids that the home-made dough is not edible.

* A thin coat of varnish will help preserve their models.

* Make clearing up part of each activity!

Chapter Two

Days Out

THE (PORTABLE) BOREDOM BOX

Use a plastic sandwich box with a lid to take with you on days out, or on holiday, as a portable boredom box. Items to add to the portable box include:

* pens and paper

* a map covering your route

* a compass

* leaflets on local attractions.

Letting the Kids Choose

A great way to plan a day out is to let your kids do it for you!

Draw up a list of possible destinations for your day out, and allow your kids to choose their favourite. Don't limit yourselves to the obvious day trips, such as theme parks and the seaside. Check the What's On section of your local newspaper, or your library for details of nearby events.

Ideas for Days Out

A few ideas for fun, and educational, days out:

* *Museums*. They often stage special children's exhibitions.

* *Airport*. Watch the planes, learn about their destinations.

* *Farms*. Spend a day with the animals.

* *Nature trails*. Explore the woods along an organised trail.

* *Fruit picking*. Get messy, and take home a basket of fruit!

* *City walks*. Learn all about your town's history.

* *Nature and bird reserves*. Watch the wildlife.

* ***Boat and canal trips***. Messing about on the water.

* ***Craft fairs***. Try your hand at arts and crafts.

* ***Pony trekking***. Saddle up, and hit the trail.

If you have an Internet connection, check out *www.kidsevents.co.uk* and *www.planit4 kids.com* for events and more suggestions for days out near you.

Your kids can use maps to plan the route, and find points of interest to stop at along the way. They can also research the chosen destination using the Internet, or leaflets from your local library or tourist information office.

Magical Mystery Tour

If you can't decide where to go, and are travelling by car – take your own Magical Mystery Tour!

Choose an area to start from on the map, and head there. Don't forget to take the map with you, and a compass too, if you have one.

When you're at your start location, each person in turn makes a decision as to where to go on the next section of the journey. By deciding that you will take 'the third turning on the right', 'the fifth turning on the left', or 'head north for six miles', you can explore the area while having absolutely no idea where you are! Jot each instruction down as you take it,

so you can find your way back again.

Chances are you'll come across shops, cafés and attractions that you wouldn't have found had you planned the route in advance. Stop as often as you can to get out and explore.

At the end of the day, reverse your route, or find a landmark and use the map to navigate your way home again.

Make Your Mark

One of the great features about days out to stately homes, castles and museums is that they frequently have a guest book for you to sign to say how you enjoyed your day. Your kids can enter their names into the book, and put the date they visited, creating a permanent record for other guests to read.

Some attractions, such as museums, will allow them to add their drawings, paintings or stories to the exhibitions for future visitors to enjoy.

Get on the Net

Another way for your kids to make their mark is to get themselves seen on one of thousands of Internet webcams.

Almost every major city and tourist attraction now has a camera broadcasting images live over the Internet. If they can find where the camera is placed, your kids can be watched around the world! For example, if you're visiting London, they could be spotted on the Leicester Square webcam at:

www.camvista.com/england/london/leicsq.php3
or the London Transport Museum webcam in Covent Garden at:
www.ltmuseum.co.uk/piazzacam/piazzac.html

In Edinburgh, be seen at:
*www.camvista.com/scotland/edinburgh/capcity
.php3*
or if you're in the Highlands, try the Loch
Ness cams at:
www.lochness.scotland.net/camera.cfm
where there's even an underwater cam to
watch for the monster! Use a search
engine to find a camera near your
destination.

If you have family in other countries with Internet connections, send them an e-mail telling them what time your kids will be posing for the camera. Use a marker pen to write a greeting on a large sheet of paper, hold it up to the camera, and say hello across the world wide web!

Pooh Cards

Wherever you go on your day out, you'll find somewhere that sells postcards with images of local attractions. Here's a great way for your kids to race them home in a contest inspired by the famous game, 'Pooh Sticks'.

Each player chooses a postcard, and addresses it to themselves, adding a message of good luck for the journey. Gather around a post box and, on a count of three, drop the cards through the slot at the same time.

Back at home, your kids can watch for the following day's post to see which card arrives first. If the postcards are racing to different addresses, a quick telephone call to the other players when their card arrives will confirm their win.

Should the cards be delivered at exactly the same time, whichever card hits the mat first will be the winner. If the title is still undecided, the time and date of the postmark can be used as a tiebreaker.

If they still can't tell who has won, declare the contest a draw, and wait until the next day out for a Pooh Cards rematch!

HINTS AND TIPS

* Alternate who chooses the destination for your days out.

* See the next chapter, 'Getting There', for ideas to make the journey fly by!

* Back at home, your kids can write and draw about their day.

Chapter Three

Getting There

THE (PORTABLE) BOREDOM BOX

- pens and paper.

Are we there yet?

One of the most boring elements of days
out is the journey. Whether travelling by
car, train or bus, the dullness factor can

be high. Time for some minimum preparation quick fixes to make that journey fly by!

Sound Effect Stories

This is one best reserved for the car, unless you want some strange looks from other train passengers!

One of the group tells a story. It can be a famous fairy tale, or a story they make up as they go along. The plot isn't the important part – the sound effects are. Your kids must fill in these sound effects as they occur in the story, using nothing but their voices.

For example, if you were telling a tale of a pirate, sailing the seven seas in search

of treasure, every time you mentioned the sea, your children would make the noise of the waves crashing against the ship. Then there's the sound of cutlasses clashing, parrots squawking, cannons firing, and so on.

Choose a story with plenty of potential for weird and wonderful noises – and don't forget your earplugs!

The Yes/No Game

A fast and furious game that can be played anywhere.

One player asks a series of questions for one minute, which the other player must answer without using the words 'yes' or 'no'. Sounds easy? Try it and see!

Ask questions such as 'What is your name?' and follow up with, 'Are you sure?'. Try 'Do you have any brothers?', 'Do you get on?' – anything that requires a 'yes' or 'no' answer.

If the player answers with either of the forbidden words, or hesitates in any way for too long, they have lost, and the points go to the question master. If they can manage a minute's grilling without saying 'yes' or 'no', the points are theirs.

Play then swaps over, and it's the question master's turn to face the challenge!

The Registration Game

This is a game to play either in the car, or when travelling by bus.

One player chooses a topic, for example 'animals'. All players must then watch the registration plates of passing cars, and note the groups of three letters displayed. The challenge is to come up with a three-word phrase relating to the topic, using those three letters as initials. So, if a car with the registration L224 DGG passes by, you could have 'Dirty Great Gorilla' or 'Donkeys Go Grey'.

Change the topic every so often, and award points for the most inventive phrases.

Quick on the Draw

If you have a hard surface to lean on, such as a table or a book, this is a giggle-filled way to pass the time.

Each player folds a sheet of paper into three, then opens it out so that the creases are still visible.

Players then draw a head in the top third, making sure that the neck stops at the first crease. The head can be anything: animal, human, alien – or a mixture of all three!

Once the head is complete, fold the paper backwards at the first crease, so that the head is hidden. Then swap the papers around, and it's up to another player to draw a body in the middle section.

Once this is done, it is also folded over, and passed to another player to draw the legs and feet.

When finished, open the paper out to admire the final creation – whatever it turns out to be!

Awful Authors

Same as the activity above, only this time the first player writes the first paragraph of a story, and folds the paper over so that only the last line of the paragraph is showing.

The next player must read that line, try to guess what the story is about, and write the next paragraph.

Once again, the paper is folded over so that only the last line of this paragraph is showing, and passed on for completion.

When each player has added their contribution, open out the papers and read the stories aloud.

Car Snooker

This isn't as crazy as it sounds – and you won't have to worry about balls rolling under the seats.

Each player has a piece of paper and a pen, and chooses a letter that has been used as the registration letter for cars within the last ten years. For example: T, V and P.

Players must watch the passing traffic for cars which are registered with their letter.

Following the rules of snooker, they need first to spot a red car with their registration letter for 1 point, then a car of another colour for an additional score:

yellow car – *2 points*

green car – *3 points*

brown car – *4 points*

blue car – *5 points*

pink (or white) car – *6 points*

black car – *7 points*

Each player has five red cars to spot (or 'pot'), and after each they must find a car of another colour from the list. Players can choose whether to accept the first car with their registration letter that comes along, or to wait for a colour with a higher value. But they mustn't wait too long, or someone else might clear the table before them!

Once they have spotted five reds and colours, they must then go through the colours in turn, from yellow to black. As there aren't that many pink cars around, they can include white cars for 6 points as well.

As they spot each car, shout out its colour so that other players know how far ahead (or behind) they are.

When one player has spotted all possible cars, everyone adds up their total number of points to find the winner. It might not be the player that finishes first.

HINTS AND TIPS

* Keep games short and plentiful on long journeys.

* Listen to music or read between games to spread them out.

* Let your kids choose which games they'd prefer to play.

Chapter Four

Holidays

THE (PORTABLE) BOREDOM BOX

* pieces of card

* sheets of blank paper

* pens and coloured pencils

* scissors

* glue

* stapler

* notepad and envelopes.

Bored on holiday?

As unlikely as it may seem, boredom can strike just as easily while you're away on holiday. Get your attack in first, with these valuable vacation ventures!

Make a Scrapbook

What better way for your children to look back at their holiday than with a personalised scrapbook, containing pictures, leaflets, diary entries, and much more? They're fun to make too!

Your kids should cut two pieces of card a little larger than A4 to use as the scrapbook's covers. Place sheets of paper between these covers, and staple down one side to keep them in place. Use at least two sheets of paper for each day of the holiday to make sure they have plenty of space to fill.

Now they can decorate the covers of their scrapbook, using coloured pencils, or by glueing items such as postcards of the holiday destination on to the front cover.

Filling The Scrapbook

One of the best ways to use the scrapbook is as a holiday diary. Each day your kids can write about what they did, where they went, and what they saw. They can stick in reminders of the day, such as train tickets, photographs, leaflets – in fact anything they can find that will remind them of the places they have visited.

Filling in the scrapbook can be an ideal way to round off each day, and adding tomorrow's date to the next blank page will have them eager to start again in the morning.

When they return home, they'll have a personalised account of their holiday to look back on, and to show friends and family.

The Holiday Hunt

Do your kids know all about the area they're staying in? Does your chosen destination have a hidden past? Are there secrets to be found?

The Holiday Hunt will give your kids the opportunity to research a specific topic – and have fun into the bargain. This activity can be run alongside the holiday scrapbook (if so, add extra pages to the scrapbook when creating it), or separately using a notepad.

Choose Your Topics

This activity will require a little research on your part before setting off on holiday. Your local library and the Internet can be useful resources for finding suitable topics for the hunt.

For this example, I've chosen the city of Lisbon in Portugal, but the same can be done for any holiday destination.

I've found three possible topics for the hunt:

* Lisbon's trams

* St George's Castle

* Statues and monuments.

Sample List

Once your child has chosen one of the topics to follow, you'll need to draw up a hunt list for the holiday, which can be stapled inside the scrapbook or notepad for easy reference.

Here are some suggestions for a sample list, and how each item is 'found' for the Lisbon trams topic:

Five facts – *2 points each*
1 – trams use 900mm gauge
2 – first trams pulled by mules
3 – first electric tram in 1901

Pictures – *3 points each*
stuck inside notepad

Visit – *10 points*
ride on a tram!

News item – *5 points*
article in local newspaper

Story – *6 points*
write about runaway tram!

Tickets – *2 points*
saved from tram journey

Drawing – *5 points*
inside scrapbook

Maps – *7 points*
tram guide, and city plan

... and so on until you have a long list for your kids to complete.

The Holiday Hunt is best followed over the entire course of your holiday, rather than as one single activity. Your

kids can carry their notepads with them
on days out to jot down any facts and
figures they may come across about their
chosen topic.

And of course, they'll be educated
without even knowing it!

Postcards Home

A great holiday tradition is to send postcards to friends and family, telling them what a great time you're having. But simply writing the cards and dropping them in the post box isn't exactly exciting.

Here are a few postcard quick fixes to liven things up!

Make Your Own!

Why buy cards that never look like the places you've visited, when your kids can make their own mail masterpieces?

They should start with a piece of blank card about 16cm by 10cm, or drop a bought postcard into a blank envelope to give it some rigidity, and stick the flap down. Draw a vertical line down the centre of one side – the recipient's name and stamp will go on the right, and the holiday greeting on the left. Be sure to leave room for both. Turn the card over, and now the artistry begins.

Quick On The Draw

This method is the easiest. Your kids can take their cards out with them to sketch an image, and leave the colouring in for an evening or rainy afternoon. If they're using paints, make sure the card is completely dry before posting!

Holiday Collage

This is a great way to show everyone at home exactly what they've been up to. Over the course of the holiday, while collecting items to stick in their scrapbooks, your kids can save a few smaller items such as tickets, receipts and stamps. When they have enough, they can form a collage on the card and glue everything securely in place.

In The Picture!

This method is a lot of fun! Choose one of the more boring postcards sold locally, and a few old photos of the family. Carefully using scissors, your kids can cut around the pictures of family members, and glue them onto the background. Use photos in a different scale from the image on the card, and add some speech bubbles with messages for everyone at home.

Postal Puzzles

If your kids would like to give their friends
a little challenge before they find out what
a great time they're having – then create a
postal puzzle.

When they have made their cards and
written their messages, they can carefully
cut the card into different sized and
shaped pieces. Drop the pieces inside an
envelope, seal it, give it a good shake, and
send the card home to be reassembled.

Don't cut the card into too many
pieces, or their friends will still be trying
to solve the puzzle long after they have
arrived home. Between 12 and 20 pieces
should keep them busy for a while.

Wish You Were Here?

Time for budding TV presenters and journalists to shine as your kids make their own holiday documentary! This activity can be tied in with the Holiday Hunt, or the daily diary in the scrapbook.

Lights, Camera, Action!

If you have access to a video camera while on holiday, then your kids can use this to shoot their own 15-minute film about your holiday destination.

If a video camera is unavailable, they can use a still camera to take shots, and write their very own travel magazine article about what visitors to the resort can expect to find.

81

Don't worry if you have neither – your kids can cut pictures from a holiday brochure, or draw sketches, for the article.

Write The Script

Their first job is to write the script, or if they're putting together a magazine article, the text that will attract visitors to their favourite holiday location.

They can talk about the journey – whether they had to fly, or came by car or train. They can explain about where they're staying. If it's a hotel, are the rooms comfortable? What is the food like?

Don't let them forget to mention local attractions. If they've had a great day out, write about it in a way that will make others want to make the same trip.

It doesn't all have to be good, however. If there's been something they don't like about their holiday – now is the time to dish the dirt!

Get Their Good Side

Here's the fun part! Now your kids can film themselves reading their script in the locations they've talked about. Or, if they're hot on the magazine trail, take pictures, or draw sketches.

It's In The Can

Back at home, your kids can edit their video by linking the camera up to a video recorder, and searching for the bits they want to keep. Play them through the video recorder, and hit the record button to capture the sections onto a blank tape in the right order. When they've finished, your kids can decorate the video cassette box with a photograph of themselves on location!

Hot Off The Press

If they've been compiling a travel article,
your kids should now dig out the text they
wrote, and cut it into smaller sections of a
few paragraphs at a time. Next, do the
same for any photographs or drawings.

Now, they can take a blank sheet of
paper, the larger the better, and glue the
text and pictures to the page. They can
draw their own travel magazine title at the
top and photocopy the article to hand out
to friends.

HINTS AND TIPS

* Your kids should keep a notebook with them in case inspiration strikes for their scrapbook or documentary.

* Get an extra set of holiday photos printed to use with their projects.

* See Chapter Two, 'Days Out' and Chapter Five, 'Stuck In Bed' for more postcard ideas!

* Dub music and a voice-over track onto the documentary in Chapter Six, 'Young Techies'.

Chapter Five

Stuck In Bed

THE BOREDOM BOX

* paper and pencils

* a tray of miscellaneous items

* old magazines and family photos

* scissors

* glue

* a candle.

Not Feeling Well?

One of the most boring situations for kids is lying in bed, recuperating from an illness. They've read all their books, listened to all their CDs, and watched television until they can stand no more. What now?

Never fear – here's a selection of quick fix activities designed with poorly patients in mind. Each can be stopped if your kids need to rest, and continued later.

Nurse – the laughing gas!

The Alphabet Game

To prepare for this game, you need to cut
up 26 squares of paper, and write a letter
of the alphabet on each (or use letters
from a Scrabble set if you have one).
Drop the letters into a bag, and give each
player a pencil and paper.

Next, choose five categories that you
will use during the game, such as 'Boys'
Names', 'Countries', 'Food', 'TV
Programmes' and 'Football Teams'. Divide
your sheet of paper into five columns, and
write the names of your categories across
the top.

One player reaches into the bag, and
pulls out a letter. Everyone then has one
minute to write down something for each

category that begins with that letter. For example, if the letter chosen is 'C', the categories above could be filled in with 'Chris', 'Cuba', 'Cakes', 'Coronation Street' and 'Chelsea'.

When one player has filled in all their categories, they shout 'Stop!' and all players must stop writing, whether they have completed their list or not.

Two points are awarded for each category correctly filled, or one point if more than one person chose the same item in the same category – so it's wise to go for more unusual answers.

The letter is then dropped back into the bag, another chosen, and play continues until the sheets of paper are full.

Photo Story

Provide your kids with a pile of old magazines and photos, some paper, scissors and glue. The aim of this activity is for your kids to cut pictures from the magazines and photographs, and glue them to the paper in the style of a photo story or comic strip. They can write the story through narration, and add speech balloons to bring the characters to life.

Why not tie the story in with the theme of their points club? Or invent an exciting tale of adventure involving friends and family?

When the story is complete, fix the sheets together, and add a cover page to create a comic of their own.

The Memory Game

A quick-fire observation game.

Prepare a tray with up to twenty household items. Cover the tray with a cloth until the game starts. When play begins, remove the cloth, and give your kids one minute to study the items. When the time is up, replace the cloth. Your kids now have one minute to recall as many of the items as they can. For each item correctly remembered, two points will be added to their points book.

Now, secretly remove one of the items, mix the rest up on the tray, and remove the cloth again. Ten points if they can spot which item is missing within ten seconds!

The Secret Code

Your kids will want their friends to know
how they're feeling, but may not want
prying eyes to read their secret messages.
The answer is to use a code.

On a sheet of paper, they should write
out the alphabet. Underneath the
alphabet, write a secret code word or
phrase, where each letter is used only
once. Here, we're using STUCK IN BED.

A B C D E F G H I J K L M N O P Q R S
S T U C K I N B E D A F G H J LMO P

T U V W X Y Z
Q R V W X Y Z

Now, they can fill in the rest of the letters that they haven't used, in alphabetical order.

To write messages in their secret code, your kids simply choose the letters from the alphabet, and use the new letter directly below. So QUICK FIXES FOR BORED KIDS becomes:

MREUA IEXKP IJO TJOKC AECP

Remember that the person they are sending the note to will need to know what the secret phrase is in order to decipher their messages.

Secret Messages

If they want to make their letter even harder to decode, your kids can write with invisible ink!

Use the end of a plain candle to write on a sheet of white paper. The writing will be impossible to read. To reveal the message, gently shade over the writing with a pencil, and the writing will magically appear.

Remember to destroy the evidence afterwards!

HINTS AND TIPS

*   Remember to supervise younger children when they are cutting pictures out of magazines.

*   Use a knife to 'sharpen' the end of a candle, to make it easier for your kids to write with.

Chapter Six

Young Techies

THE BOREDOM BOX

* sheets of paper and pens

* a VCR or cassette deck

* a blank video or audio cassette

* various props for making sound effects.

We have the technology

No matter how much you object, your kids will still spend a good deal of their time glued to the TV set, playing video games, or surfing the Internet.

With so much technology at hand these days, it makes sense to embrace it. Here are a few quick fixes that will not only allow them to use their favourite gadgets – but adds a sneaky element of education into the fun too.

I won't tell them if you don't!

Online Fun

If you have access to the Internet, there's a whole world of educational activities to keep your kids amused.

Bear in mind that, at the time of writing, most Internet access in the UK is charged at local rates on your telephone bill, so keep an eye on the amount of time they spend online.

Taking Precautions

As you are no doubt aware, there is a less savoury side to the Internet. However, it isn't as prolific as the media would have us believe and, with a few simple precautions, it is simple for your children to avoid.

A good way is to install filtering software. This automatically blocks access to sites which don't pass strict guidelines, and allows you to add access rules of your own. Several different software packages are available. Two of the most popular are Cybersitter (*www.cybersitter.com*) and NetNanny (*www.netnanny.com*). More information can be found at their websites.

Whether or not you decide to use filtering software, it is important that your children know never to give out personal details, such as their address or telephone number, over the Internet.

Internet Hunt

Here's a great way for your kids to spend 30 minutes surfing from site to site, and pick up a little knowledge along the way.

Prepare an Internet Hunt list with items that your kids must find within the time limit. These could include:

* the website address for the White House – *2 points*

* a site that has a map of London – *3 points*

* 3 different webcams – *4 points each*

* a site about a pop group – *1 point*

* a recipe from the Internet – *3 points*

* the Prime Minister's email address – *10 points*

* 3 facts about the Amazon jungle –
  3 points each

* a picture of a Porsche – *5 points*

Add as many items as you can to the list, and let them loose for a session of cyber hunting!

E-Pals

A great way to learn about different countries and cultures is by writing to a pen pal, and email makes it easier than ever.

If you have an Internet account, you may be able to add different aliases to your email address for your kids to use. If not, they can get a free email address at Hotmail (*www.hotmail.com*) or Yahoo (*http://mail.yahoo.com*). These can be accessed from any computer with an Internet connection – perfect if they send their email from the local library or Internet café.

Where To Find Pen Pals

It is important that you screen any pen pal sites that your child visits. Don't pay for addresses, and make sure that your child writes to pen pals of a suitable age. Good sites to start at include:

* Penpal Listings
  www.geocities.com/SouthBeach/Surf/6636/index.html

* Penpal Box
  www.ks-connection.org/penpal/penpal.html

Square Eyes!

If your kids are forever in front of the TV or video, here are a couple of quick fixes that won't drag them away!

Video Dub

If you have a video recorder that allows you to plug in a microphone and dub a new soundtrack onto a video cassette, they have the opportunity for hours of hilarious fun.

If your VCR doesn't have this facility, don't worry. They can turn the volume down on the TV, record a new soundtrack on a cassette player, and play it back in sync with the video.

Your kids should choose a film or TV show that they've watched more than once (and one that they don't want to keep if they're dubbing straight onto the tape).

Set the counter to zero on the VCR, and on the cassette player if they're using one. Time for them to take a deep breath, hit 'record' and start dubbing!

They have to ad-lib an entirely new story, and not worry too much about getting their words in sync with the actors on screen – they can always wipe the tape clean afterwards. They can improvise their own sound effects too. A few simple props can make some weird and wonderful noises.

This activity works best with a few friends around, each playing several of the characters on screen, and the end result is often more entertaining than the original version!

Soap Suds

Should your kids be soap fans, encourage
them to take their interest a step further,
and write an episode of their favourite
show. They'll already know the characters
well, and be up to date on the current
storylines – but how do they see these
domestic dramas unfolding?

Scripts can be written either in
longhand, or on a computer, and have a
few basic rules to follow:

```
INT. Ian's House - Day
```

A scene heading, like the one above, starts
with INT. (interior) or EXT. (exterior) to
show where and when the drama takes
place.

The action itself is written across the page in short paragraphs like this.

> IAN sits at his desk, wondering what to write next. DOT enters the room.

> IAN

A character's name is written in the centre of the page, with his dialogue below.

> DOT
> No time for that. Have
> you heard the news?
>
> Ian spins round in his chair.

> ### IAN
> What?
>
> ### DOT
> Pauline has just found out that Peggy is her long lost twin sister and that she owns half the pub.
>
> Ian stares at Dot in amazement.

This scene won't make it to the screen, but it shows basic script format. In this style, an A4 page of script equals roughly a minute on the screen – so for an episode of a soap opera, they'll need to complete 30 pages.

Your kids should watch a few episodes of their favourite soap to see how long each scene lasts, and how each episode ends on a cliffhanger to make them tune in next time.

The fate of the characters lies in their hands!

Game Play

If your kids are computer games buffs,
they can adapt the above activity, and
write a sequel to their favourite game.
They can invent a fresh storyline; create
new, harder levels; draw maps to each of
the locations; and design puzzles and
traps for players to solve. They'll need to
introduce some new characters, including
a stronger, tougher enemy to battle
against. They should create the game
they'd like to play next!

Radio Ga Ga

Why not get your kids to combine all of the activities above, and create their own radio play?

They can write the script – for their favourite TV show, computer game, or even an original story – create some sound effects, add music and record it all onto cassette.

Or, if they have access to a video
camera, they could shoot their own short
film. Once they have all their scenes, they
can edit them together by plugging the
camera into the VCR, finding each scene
in turn, and hitting 'record' on the video
as it plays.

Your kids can dub sound effects and
music on later, and they could even film
sheets of card with the end credits. Next
stop – the Oscars!

HINTS AND TIPS

* Check the web site of their favourite soap opera for script tips, and hints at future story lines.

* Use or make a stand for the microphone to save any unwanted noises as they pass it around.

* Take the cassette player outside to record sound effects such as traffic and birds.

Chapter Seven

All Together Now

THE BOREDOM BOX

* scavenger lists and pencils

* a soft football or beach ball

* balloons

* a secondhand parachute (trust me!)

* a whistle.

Group fun

It's all very well entertaining one or two kids, but what happens when you are required to keep a large group occupied? Maybe your loved ones have arrived home with the entire class in tow, or you're called upon to provide an evening's fun for your child's cub or brownie meeting?

Never fear – there are quick fixes for groups too!

Game On!

Two quick games, ideal for warming the group up:

Drop It!

Players stand in a circle, facing inward, with you in the centre, holding a soft football or beach ball.

Toss the ball to any player at random, and shout either 'Catch it!' or 'Drop it!' That player must quickly do the exact opposite to your command.

If you shout 'Drop it!' and the player catches the ball (correct), they toss the ball back, and remain standing. However, if they drop the ball, and match your order – they have to kneel down to continue playing. (No one is ever 'out', but only standing players can win the game.)

As play continues, speed the game up, and occasionally toss the ball to the same player twice in a row to surprise them. Don't forget to include the kneeling players.

The last player standing is declared the winner, and is awarded the points.

Pop Swap

Players sit in a circle, facing inward.

Ask the group to name three of their favourite pop bands or artists. You'll be inundated with dozens of groups, but try to pick the three simplest names for use in the game.

Moving around the circle, give each child in turn one of the band names to remember (for example, Steps, Travis, Madonna, Steps, Travis, Madonna, etc.). When each child has been assigned a name, check they know which they all are – then begin the fun.

Call out a pop name. Each child with that name must jump up, run clockwise around the outside of the circle, and sit back down in their seat. Do this several times for each name to really get the energy of the game up.

Try calling out two band names at once, and watch the chaos as two-thirds of the group rush around the room (keep an eye on any younger players in case they are knocked over).

Now the game gets difficult! From now on, players must run around the circle when their name is called, but must run past their own seat, and find another, vacant seat to sit in.

When everyone is exhausted – end the game!

Scavenger Hunt

You will need to prepare Scavenger Lists
for this hunt. Split the group into pairs
and give each team a copy of the list.

When the hunt starts, each team will
have 30 minutes to find as many items on
the Scavenger List as they can, and bring
them back to base. Each item on the list
is worth a specific number of points – the
harder the object is to find, the higher its
point value.

Be sure to stress a few simple rules:

* Set boundaries which the teams
  cannot search beyond.

* Team members must stick together at
  all times.

* Items must be carried around with the
  team.

* Don't take anything without the
  permission of its owner!

Out For The Count

When the time is up, the teams gather
at the start area, and lay out what they
have found. Go through each team's list,
calling out items in turn, which the team
must produce to earn the points. Keep a
running total of each team's points to add
to their books at the end of the game.

The Scavenger List

Below is a sample of a typical Scavenger List. Try to aim for between 40 and 50 items on the list, so that the teams don't finish too early! For more lists, visit the Bored Kids website at *www.wobblebottom .com/boredkids*

* a toothbrush – *1 point*

* a pair of glasses, but not sunglasses – *3 points*

* something that is blue and yellow – *4 points*

* a signature – 1 *point*

* a cup of water – *2 points*

* a picture of the Queen – *3 points*

* something that comes in a pair – *2 points*

* a teddy bear – *1 point*

* salt – *1 point*

* a photograph of a fish – *5 points*

* something edible – *2 points*

* a foreign coin – *6 points*

... and so on, until you have a long list for the teams to follow.

Parachute Games

If you have to entertain a large group on a regular basis, investing in a secondhand parachute (with the cords removed) is a great idea. They can be bought at army surplus stores, and will provide hours of fun.

Parachute Rules

Safety is a top concern when using a parachute, and explaining a few simple rules at the start of the session will ensure that everyone enjoys the games.

*   No one steps onto or climbs beneath the parachute without your permission.

* Anyone stepping onto or climbing
  beneath the parachute must remove
  their shoes, and any items from their
  pockets.

* Explain each game thoroughly before
  you begin.

* Carry a whistle – everything stops, and
  everyone releases their grip on the
  parachute, when you blow it.

The Games

There are dozens of possibilities for parachute games. Here are three fun suggestions:

Jellyfish

Players stand evenly spaced around the outside of the parachute, holding it by the edge.

On the count of one, the players raise their arms, billowing the parachute above their heads.

On two, everyone takes a step inward – the parachute will billow more.

On three, everyone pulls their section of parachute down behind them, and sits on it!

The parachute will pull tight over the heads of all the players, and, from the outside, it will look like a huge jellyfish! Get the kids to wobble about from side to side for extra effect.

It will get hot beneath the parachute very quickly, so don't let them stay under for too long. To get out, everyone should shuffle forward, and lift the parachute over their heads and onto their laps first.

Chute Ball

Players stand around the parachute, and hold its edges. This time, ask them to roll the edge of their section in a little until they have a better grip, and the centre of the parachute is taut.

Split the circle into two even teams, and throw a ball on top of the parachute. Wait until it comes to rest at the centre.

On your whistle, players must shake their section of the parachute to try and launch the ball over the heads of the opposite team for a goal. Keeping the parachute taut while shaking will make the ball move better.

*   Keep an eye on younger players. Make
    sure they aren't being shaken along
    with the 'chute.

*   Players cannot knock the ball back in
    with their hands if it bounces past
    them.

*   Any cheating results in a penalty to
    the opposing team: three free shakes!

The first team to score five goals wins the
game.

Jaws

No matter how many parachute games you play – this will be their favourite!

Players stand around the parachute, holding the edge tightly at waist height, with a little rolled up for grip.

One player is chosen to be the shark. That player steps beneath the parachute, and holds their hands together over their head to simulate the fin.

When the game begins, the players holding the parachute wobble it gently, turning the parachute into an undulating ocean. In unison, these players softly chant the famous 'Da-dum... Da-dum' of the *Jaws* movie theme.

Beneath the surface of the 'water', the shark begins to run around, its 'fin' pressing against the underside of the parachute.

The shaking increases as the ocean starts to get rougher, the chant gets louder, and the shark searches for a victim!

The shark must swim up to one of the players on the outside of the circle, and tap their legs. That player screams out a blood-curdling yell, and lets themself be dragged beneath the waves – where they become a second shark!

Now two sharks are circling the sea, which gets rougher by the second as the parachute is shaken harder, and the *Jaws* theme is sung louder. Watch out that younger players don't hurt their hands as the sea gets choppier.

Each shark chooses a new victim and, to the sound of more screams, they join those already beneath the waves.

When the sea is filled with sharks, blow your whistle, and let everyone out from beneath the parachute.

HINTS AND TIPS

* Explain that the sharks should never actually drag a victim beneath the parachute – just a tap on the leg, and the victim does the rest.

* Encourage the players to keep up the chant, and keep the parachute as taut as possible.

* Don't allow yourself to be dragged under by a shark (they'll all try!) Stay on the surface to keep control of the game.

Chapter Eight

The Children's Party

THE BOREDOM BOX

*   paper and coloured pens
*   sticky labels
*   two paint pots
*   a length of string or rope
*   a table
*   small prizes
*   pieces of card
*   rolls of old wrapping paper.

The Dreaded Party!

There's something very satisfying about taking a child to a party at someone else's house. Dropping them at the door, gift in hand, as chaos reigns in the background. Walking away for an hour or two, smug in the knowledge that it's not your turn ... yet!

The prospect of organising a children's party can be quite daunting. Yet, with a little planning, your kid's party will not only be a great success – it will be the one their friends will remember!

How many?

The first decision you must make is how many of your kid's friends to invite. While it is tempting to simply invite the entire class, you will be limited by how many children you can accommodate in your home for the afternoon. If you simply must invite everyone, consider hiring a local hall or function room for the party.

Invites

Once you have a number, draw up an invite list with your kid.

You now have a built-in activity! Why buy party invitations when your kid can make them? If your party is following a theme, they could design custom invitations that match.

Whether they write them by hand, or design them on a computer, make sure they're delivered in plenty of time, and attach an RSVP slip to the bottom so you have an idea of how many guests will show.

Remember to specify a start and end time to the party. Two and a half hours is a good length with games, food and entertainment.

The Big Day

Take time to set out your party room according to a few simple rules, and you'll save yourself a lot of hassle:

* Keep food covered at one end of the room, or in a separate room entirely.

* If you are booking an entertainer, reserve a space at the other end of the room, against a wall.

* Clear space for games in the centre of the room.

* Remove any breakables, or items that can cause harm, and store them away until after the party.

Here they come!

The party guests are arriving, bearing gifts, with parents in tow. But don't let them in just yet! Here are a few tips to help things run smoothly:

* As each child arrives, whether you know them well or not, attach a sticker with their name to their shirt. This will not only help you later in the party, but will break the ice with the other kids.

* Get rid of the parents! Except for those who are here to help, parents who hang around get in the way. Smile politely, and tell them what time to come back to pick up their kids.

* Save presents for later. Put another
name sticker on each gift as it arrives
saying who it is from, and open them
later in the party. This will avoid gifts
becoming lost or broken at the hands
of party guests – sometimes before
your child gets a chance to play with
them.

The Order Of The Day

The order of party events is up to you but, after entertaining at hundreds of parties over the years, here is what I recommend:

Games

Food

Entertainment

Presents

Why? Everyone arrives at a party excited, and feeling more than a little rowdy. If you try to sit the kids down to eat, or to watch a show now – they won't. Better to put that energy to use and play some games. Later, when everyone is just a little worn out, they'll be glad for the chance to have a break, and some food.

Once they've eaten, it's the perfect time to sit them down for some entertainment while their food settles. The show will build them up just enough to enjoy watching the opening of the presents, and maybe the cutting of the birthday cake too!

Party Games

If there is one quick fix, hint or tip that you take away from this chapter – let it be this one:

Do not play
musical chairs!

Here's a secret... most kids don't like the game. Even if they once did, they've played it at every single birthday, Christmas and school party they've ever been to – and it's wearing a little thin. Musical chairs is a prime example of a party game that adults think kids must love. Plus, you're the one that will have to deal with a dozen bored party guests careering around the edge of the room while two determined finalists battle it out for ownership of that last chair. It's really not worth it, trust me.

Here are three party games that don't result in anyone being 'out'.

Traffic Lights

A fast and furious game to really get the party going!

Players stand in a space in the room, arms stretched out as though clutching the steering wheel of a car. Your job is to call out the colours of a set of traffic lights – red, amber or green. When you shout red, players must stop where they are, frozen. Amber, and they must sit down, cross-legged – as though waiting for the lights to change. On green, they must 'drive' around the room, making car noises, and avoiding accidents!

That's all there is to it. Shout out the colours at random, and get faster as the game progresses. They'll sleep well tonight!

Poor Pussy

Players sit in a circle with their legs crossed. One player is chosen to be a 'cat', and must crawl around the centre of the circle.

The cat chooses a player to approach, slinks up, and offers a loud 'Meow!' to them. The chosen player must then pat the cat three times (gently) on the head and say, 'Aww... Poor Pussy!' – without laughing!

If the player laughs, giggles or even smiles, they must exchange places with the cat, and choose a victim of their own. If the player manages not to laugh, the cat moves on, and picks another player to approach.

The idea of the game is to keep the cat in the centre for as long as possible by not laughing at its feline advances. But, the better the cat, the less chance of that happening.

Pass The Pop Parcel

Not avoiding traditional games, entirely – Pass The Pop Parcel is a variation on the party favourite.

Wrap a small gift in sheets of paper (old wrapping paper works well), but in between each sheet, add a slip of card with a pop star or band's name on.

Play pass the parcel as usual (when the music stops, the player with the parcel tears off one layer of paper). In this version, however, that player must, without revealing the name on the card, either sing a snippet of one of their songs, or do an impression of the artist.

If the other guests can correctly guess the name of the pop star or band, the player wins a small prize, and play continues. If the player is a little shy, jump in and help them.

The game ends when the final sheet of paper is torn off, and one of the players wins the final prize.

Food Glorious Food

Whatever food you serve at the party, avoid the temptation to force 'healthy' foods on to the guests. While I'm not suggesting you fill them with burgers and chips, one or two sweet treats among the offerings won't hurt for one afternoon – it is a party, after all!

A buffet-style selection is easier to arrange than a full sit-down meal, and remember to ask your guests' parents for any special dietary requirements when they arrive. Write any special foods they must avoid on their name sticker so you don't forget in the rush.

That's Entertainment

One way of ensuring that your party goes
with a bang is to hire a professional
children's entertainer. Be it a clown,
magician or puppeteer, follow a few
simple tips and they'll take the party out
of your hands long enough for you to
catch your breath! Here are a few tips in
finding an entertainer:

* If you can, choose an entertainer by
  word of mouth. If they've been a
  success at another party, they'll make a
  success of yours.

* Be sure to ask exactly what they can
  provide at the party. (For example,
  some entertainers will run the party

games for an added fee. Perfect if you can't face the task yourself.)

* Give the number of children expected at the party, and their ages. This will affect the price and form of entertainment.

* Magic shows rarely work with groups of children under 5 years old – but your local entertainer may have the answer.

Showtime!

Reserve a space for the entertainment at one end of the room, against a wall. One way to section this space off is to tie a length of string between two paint tins (your kids could decorate them), and insist that nobody crosses the line.

Ensure that noone disturbs the entertainer while they set up or pack away their show. This is especially true of parents, who often feel compelled to meddle with props!

Always pay the entertainer promptly, and if you've enjoyed the show, ask for business cards to pass around to other parents.

HINTS AND TIPS

* Enlist older children to help look after youngsters at the party. It will avoid both groups feeling out of place.

* Ensure that quieter children aren't left out of the games. Remember, they're all wearing name stickers.

* When playing Pass The Pop Parcel with younger children, use pictures of animals instead of pop groups.

* Prepare party bags for guests to take home, with a few small surprises, and maybe a slice of birthday cake.

* Keep your cool – and remember to enjoy yourself too!

Chapter Nine

Abracadabra

THE BOREDOM BOX

* a piece of dowelling

* black and white paint

* a pack of cards

* silk handkerchiefs or pieces of coloured cloth

* an old ring

* a table tennis paddle

* a large piece of fabric

* needle and thread.

Magic in the Air

This chapter can be used either by parents who have decided to perform at their children's party, or handed to the kids themselves as an introduction to the world of magic.

Although the tricks contained within this chapter are easy to prepare and perform, they will require practice before being presented before an audience. Rehearse in front of a mirror to make sure that all your moves are clean, and that the mechanics of the tricks are hidden.

Remember that magicians never reveal their secrets, no matter how much the audience asks. Never perform a trick twice in a row – your audience will be watching to see how it is done the second time.

The Magic Wand

Every magician uses a magic wand, and not just for show. A wand can help you in one of the magician's greatest skills – misdirection. By using the wand to point to an object, or by waving it magically, you can divert people's attention away from the area where the real 'magic' is happening.

You can make your own wand with a 30cm length of dowelling. Paint the middle of the wand black, and the ends white. (Why? The good 'white magic' keeps the 'black magic' trapped, so it can never escape into the world!) When it is dry, you can apply a coat of varnish to prevent the paint chipping off.

The Magic Spell

You'll need a magic spell for your audience to shout out. Some magicians use 'Abracadabra' or 'Hocus Pocus', but why not come up with a magic spell of your own? Something silly like 'Iddledy Piddledy!', or 'Umpah Lumpah!' will get a laugh. Keep it simple, so that your audience will remember it.

Now, let's learn some tricks!

Five Alive!

From an ordinary pack of cards, pull out
four cards at random, and a '5' card (it
doesn't matter which one).

With the pack face down, place the 5
card face up at the bottom of the pack, and
the other four cards face down below it.

To perform the trick, fan the cards
slightly (without showing the 5 card), and
ask your volunteer to choose a card
without showing you, and remember it.

While they are looking at their card,
straighten the pack up and place it face
down on the table. Now, ask your
volunteer to put their card face down on
top of the deck, and cut the pack. Now,
their chosen card, and your 5 card, are in

the middle of the pack somewhere.

Tell your audience that your magic number is 5, and ask them to count to 5 with you... 1, 2, 3, 4, 5! On the number 5, slam your hand down hard on top of the pack.

Now spread the cards out from left to right, and point out that one of the cards, a number 5, has turned itself over in the pack to help you find your volunteer's card. Make a big show of counting left 5 cards, and flip that card over to reveal it is the one your volunteer chose!

The Magic Bag

To make a magic bag, you'll need two pieces of dark coloured fabric – one approximately 40cm by 25cm, and one 20cm by 25cm.

Lay the larger piece on the table, and mark a line down the centre, at 20cm along. Sew the edge of the smaller piece along this line. Now, fold the large piece over, and sew all three pieces together up at both sides. You should end up with a bag with two separate pockets. You can add stars or sequins to it to make it look magical.

To use the bag, hide four silk handkerchiefs, or coloured pieces of thin cloth, inside one side of the bag. Show your audience that the bag is empty, by pushing the other side of the bag inside out.

Push the bag back the right way, and wave your magic wand. Reach into the secret compartment, and pull out a coloured handkerchief.

Repeat the trick three more times, each time showing the audience that the bag is empty, and 'produce' a coloured silk from the secret pocket.

Now you can put the handkerchiefs back into the bag, wave your wand, and make them all disappear again.

Disappearing Ring

To perform this trick, you'll need to make your own magic handkerchief. For this, you'll need a piece of fabric around 40cm by 20cm, and an old ring (a plastic toy ring will do).

Divide the cloth in half, 20cm along, and fix the ring into the middle of one of the halves with a small stitch or two, making sure the stitches don't show from the other side.

Now, fold the cloth over, and stitch all around the sides, so that the ring is hidden inside the handkerchief. Use an iron to press the edges flat.

For the trick, borrow a ring from a lady in the audience, making a big deal about how expensive it is.

Show the audience your handkerchief from both sides, and drape it over the ring in your hand. Hide the real ring in the palm of your hand, and with your other hand, grasp the fake ring hidden inside the handkerchief, and lift it up.

Reach over to your table for your magic wand, and drop the real ring behind another prop, such as your magic bag, when you pick up the wand.

You can ask members of the audience to feel the 'ring' beneath the handkerchief to prove it is still there (they're really touching your fake ring). Now wave your wand, cast your spell and, to the amazement of everyone, pull the handkerchief away. The ring has vanished!

You can make the ring reappear by using your magic bag. Just drop it into the secret compartment as you reach over to pick the bag up.

Magic Table Tennis

For this trick you'll need a table tennis paddle (or another type of bat with a solid face). You'll also need to learn how to 'force' a card.

Choose one card from a pack, for example the 6 of diamonds, and stick it to one side of the bat (fold over a couple of pieces of sticky tape). Place the rest of the pack on the table.

For the trick, pick a volunteer from the audience, and ask them to hold the pack of cards in their hand. Now you have to get them to 'choose' the card you have stuck to the bat. It's not as hard as it sounds!

Explain that there are four suits in a

pack of cards – hearts, diamonds, clubs and spades. Ask them to choose any two of the suits, and tell you which ones they have picked. Remember you are aiming for the 6 of diamonds.

If your volunteer chooses diamonds as one of their suits, (perhaps they pick hearts and diamonds), move on to the next section. If they don't, and for example choose clubs and spades, simply say, 'OK, let's get rid of them, and that leaves hearts and diamonds'. Always keep diamonds.

Now, ask them to choose one suit
from the remaining two – hearts and
diamonds. Again, if they choose
diamonds, move on. If not, get rid of
their choice, hearts, leaving diamonds!

Choose four cards at 'random' which
cover your card's number, perhaps the 4,
5, 6 and 7 of diamonds. Ask your
volunteer to choose two. If they choose
the 6 and another card, move on. If the 6
isn't in their choice, get rid of them, and
tell them what they have left.

From the remaining two cards, ask
them to pick one. If they pick the 6,
you've done it. If not, tell them you're
getting rid of that card, which leaves the 6
of diamonds. Your volunteer thinks they
have chosen a card at random!

Now take the pack of cards from their hand, and grab the bat from the table, making sure that the card is hidden from the audience.

Hit the pack of cards with the bat as hard as you can, scattering them over the heads of your audience. As they scream and duck, quickly flip the bat over.

When the audience looks back, they'll see that the chosen card has magically stuck itself to the bat!

HINTS AND TIPS

* For more tricks, find your local magic shop (check the telephone directory).

* Check your library for books of magic.

* Most towns have a magic club you can join to learn more.

* Practise, practise, practise!

Chapter Ten

You Must Be Joking!

THE BOREDOM BOX

* pens and paper
* needle and thread
* a 20p coin
* glue
* food colouring.

The Joke's on You!

Your kids can while away a few hours by writing their own jokes, limericks and poems. Or they could surprise their friends with a few practical jokes.

Show them the examples in this chapter, and they'll soon be creating their own routines.

Knock Knock!

Knock Knock jokes have been favourites
for years! Here's a few to get you started –
see how many you can come up with.

> Knock Knock!
> Who's there?
> Tish
> Tish who?
> Use a handkerchief when
> you sneeze!

Knock Knock!
Who's there?
Yule
Yule who?
Yule never know unless
you open the door!

Knock Knock!
Who's there?
Sarah
Sarah who?
Sarah 'nother way to
get in?

Is there a Doctor in the House?

Doctor, Doctor jokes are great fun! Tell them in two parts – one line from the 'patient', and a reply from the doctor. Can you come up with any of your own like these?

~ Doctor, Doctor – I feel like a kangaroo!
  Hop it!

~ Doctor, Doctor – people keep ignoring me!
  Next please!

~ Doctor, Doctor – I just swallowed a pound coin!
  Come back tomorrow if there's any change!

What's in a Name?

Here are a few gigglesome gags based around people's names. See if you can come up with one about your name...

~ What do you call a man in a brown envelope?
Bill!

~ What do you call a woman in a strong wind?
Gale!

~ What do you call a man in a pile of leaves?
Russell!

What do you get... ?

What do you get if you cross these jokes with your friends? Lots of laughs! Try them out...

~ What do you get if you cross a sheep and a kangaroo?
   A woolly jumper!

~ What do you get if you cross a dog with a hairdresser?
   A shampoodle!

~ What do you get if you cross a kangaroo with an elephant?
   Big holes all over Australia!

Can you come up with some more?

The Verse Is Worse!

Another way of getting laughs is to write your own silly poetry. Keep the verses short, and make sure they rhyme. Here's a few yucky poems to get you going...!

I put my goldfish on the floor
He isn't very fit.
He only did ten sit-ups
Then lay still, that was it.

My sister said of her new flat,
'There's not enough room to swing a cat.'
So I asked my Grandma, 'Please
May I borrow your Siamese?'
I swung it round with all my might
And do you know, my sister's right!

Or you could set them out in Limerick
form...

There one was a fairy called Nuff
Who went round the town acting tough.
To jail he was sent
This bad fairy gent
And everyone said, 'Fairy Nuff!'

Practical Jokes

If you're feeling particularly wicked, you could play a few practical jokes on your friends – but don't make them too awful, or they won't stay friends for long! Here are a couple to try out...

Stitched Up

You'll need to get access to your victim's socks, and have a needle and thread handy. Put a few stitches half-way down each sock (not too tightly, you don't want to ruin them!) Sit back and giggle as they struggle to get their feet inside!

Funny Money

Take a 20p coin, and glue it to the pavement outside your house. Watch from a window as passers-by spot the coin, and try their hardest to pick it up!

Monstrous Milk

Tell your friends that farmers have found a way to breed multi-coloured cows. When they don't believe you, open the fridge, take out a carton of milk and pour them a glass of red, green, or blue milk! In secret you've added a few drops of food colouring to the milk, and gently shaken it. The colourful milk is perfectly safe to drink.

HINTS AND TIPS

* If no one laughs at your jokes, don't worry. Everyone has a different sense of humour. Just keep writing them.

* Don't play practical jokes that will hurt or scare people, or damage property.